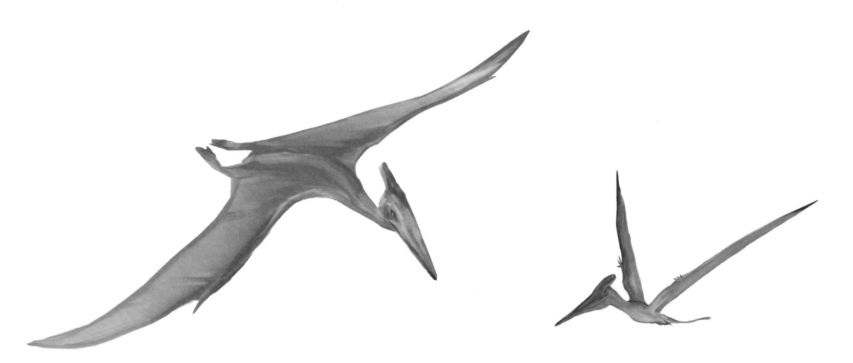

The AGE of DINOSAURS

TABLE of CONTENTS

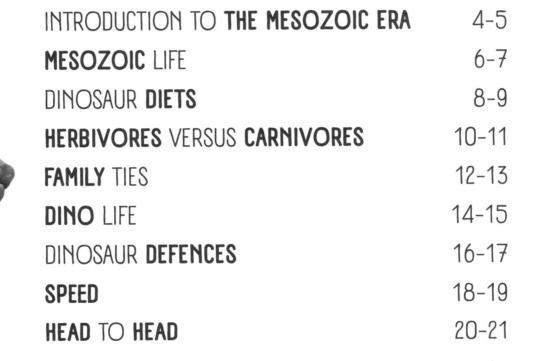

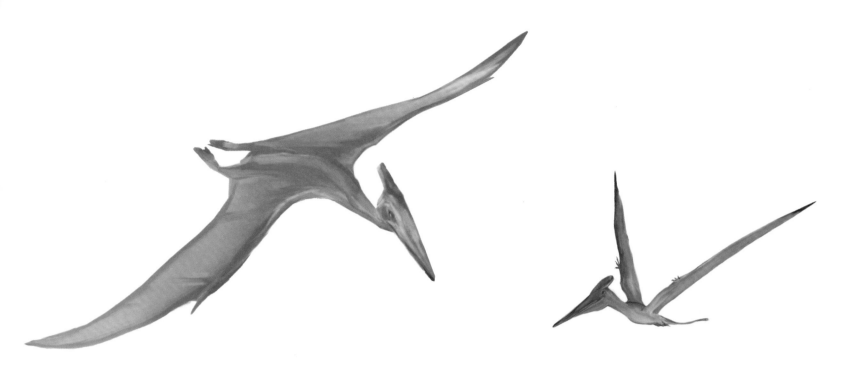

INTRODUCTION TO
THE MESOZOIC ERA

The Mesozoic Era is the name for the period on Earth that ran from 252 million years ago until 66 million years ago. It is the period that saw the dinosaurs emerge... and disappear again.

THE MESOZOIC **CLIMATE**

Earth's climate during this period was generally warm, without the big difference in temperature we find between the Equator and the poles today. This created the ideal conditions for all sorts of new life forms to emerge. Since there was no polar ice, the sea level was higher than it is today.

mya = million years ago

Triassic Period	**Jurassic** Period	**Cretaceous** Period
252 mya	201 mya	145 mya 66 mya

TIMELINE

The Mesozoic Era can be broken down into three distinct phases: the first of these was the Triassic Period (252 to 201 million years ago), then came the Jurassic (201 to 145 million years ago) and, finally, the Cretaceous (145 to 66 million years ago).

MOUNTAINS HIGH

Although the continents have continued to shift slowly over time, Earth had already begun to resemble the planet we know today by the close of the Cretaceous Period. Even some still existing mountain ranges thrust upwards during the Mesozoic Era.

Pangea: 252 mya

A SINGLE **SUPER-CONTINENT**

At the beginning of the Mesozoic Era, all of Earth's continents were joined together in one enormous 'super-continent' known as Pangea. However, an increase in volcanic and seismic (earthquake) activity towards the end of the Triassic Period caused fractures to appear. Then, during the Jurassic, North America and – further south – Africa, South America and Australia gradually pulled away from the main continental mass.

THE AGE OF **THE DINOSAURS**

Dinosaurs roamed Earth from the late stages of the Triassic (around 230 million years ago) until the cataclysmic event that brought about their downfall at the end of the Cretaceous Period some 66 million years ago. These incredible terrestrial creatures came in all shapes and sizes and co-existed with a number of other animals, including the plesiosaurs and pterosaurs.

MESOZOIC LIFE

The word 'dinosaur' comes from the Ancient Greek words 'deinos' (terrible) and 'sauros' (lizard). While dinosaurs have always been classified as reptiles, they are not actually the ancestors of today's snakes and lizards. Yet if you go back far enough, the dinosaurs do share a common ancestor with modern-day reptiles, as well as with mammals.

THE DIFFERENCE BETWEEN DINOSAURS AND OTHER REPTILES

The dinosaurs shared many characteristics with modern-day reptiles. For example, they hatched from eggs and had scales. However, unlike today's cold-blooded reptiles, the dinosaurs were probably warm-blooded. This means that they were able to regulate their own body temperature and did not rely on the sun to keep warm.

DID DINOSAURS LIVE ALL OVER THE PLANET?

When the dinosaurs first appeared, there was only one continent. The oldest known species was found in modern-day Argentina, but dinosaurs are likely to have lived all over the enormous land mass. Indeed, dinosaur fossils have been found in every single one of our continents… but many of their species seem to have stuck to a specific region.

OTHER ANIMAL LIFE

The dinosaurs were not alone on Earth. Their prehistoric cousins included the pterosaurs (including the pterodactyl) in the skies above and the marine-based plesiosaurs. Some of the creatures that lived alongside the dinosaurs will be even more familiar to us – they include shrew-like creatures, bees, snakes, lizards, crocodiles and sharks!

GREEN **PLANET**

As the continents began to divide up, this created smaller seas and increased the rainfall on land. This in turn allowed green plants to thrive, providing a plentiful food supply for herbivorous dinosaurs, which began to dominate the landscape during the Jurassic Period. Flowering plants appeared for the first time during the Cretaceous Period. Up until then, the world was not a very colourful place!

MASS EXTINCTIONS

At the dawn of the Mesozoic, over 250 million years ago, our planet suffered one of its greatest 'mass extinctions', with around 9 in every 10 marine invertebrates and 7 in 10 land vertebrates disappearing off the face of the Earth. This was followed by another mass extinction at the end of the Triassic Period, in which many land animals were wiped out... but not the dinosaurs!

END OF **AN ERA**

But dino robustness was put to the ultimate test 66 million years ago when a massive meteorite measuring over 10 kilometres across hit Earth off the coast of Mexico. A huge dust cloud billowed up into the atmosphere, blocking out a lot of the planet's sunlight. This kickstarted a chain reaction: the plants died, which meant the herbivores died, which in turn meant the end of the carnivores. This time there was no escape!

DINOSAUR **DIETS**

What a dinosaur ate depended entirely on what kind of dinosaur it was. Like the animals on Earth today, some prehistoric creatures were vegetarian, others preferred their meat and others still ate whatever they could get their claws on!

HERBIVORES

The herbivores did not evolve until the Jurassic Period, when plant life began to flourish on Earth. Only now was there enough food to sustain them. There is evidence that the stomachs of some of the largest herbivores contained stones and microbes that helped to break down the tough plant matter they were endlessly needing to consume to maintain their huge bulk. These dinosaurs did not have – or require – the razor-sharp teeth of their predatory cousins.

OMNIVORES

A few dinosaurs did not restrict themselves to one type of food, but could instead survive on a mixture of meat and vegetables, just as we can. One such dinosaur was Oviraptor, the wrongly accused 'egg thief'. Oviraptor's toothless jaws were so strong that they would have been able to crack open hard objects such as clams and hard fruits, and it may also have eaten small lizards and plants.

BIG APPETITES

As a general rule, the bigger the dinosaur, the bigger its appetite! What is surprising, though, is that the very biggest dinosaurs of all, such as Argentinosaurus and Brachiosaurus, survived on an entirely plant-based diet. They therefore posed no threat to the dinosaurs they lived alongside – unlike T-Rex, who gobbled up smaller dinosaurs without mercy.

CARNIVORES

Tyrannosaurus Rex, or T-Rex, was probably the most notorious of the meat-eaters. With a voracious appetite and extremely large, sharp teeth to rip apart its prey, T-Rex would have made all but the very biggest herbivores quake in their boots! Its teeth were regularly replaced when they became worn down, much like crocodiles' teeth today. However, not all carnivores were as big. Compsognathus was a very small, very fast dinosaur that was nippy enough to catch lizards to eat.

HERBIVORES
VERSUS
CARNIVORES

HERBIVORES

BRAIN
Often very small in comparison with the size of their body.

MOUTH
Flat, blunt teeth designed for chewing, with a side-to-side, scissor-like jaw action. Some herbivores didn't even chew their food – they simply swallowed it and let it break down in their stomachs!

NECK
Many herbivorous dinosaurs evolved extremely long necks – far out of proportion with their bodies – so that they could reach up into the tallest trees, so reducing their chances of going hungry.

SIZE AND AGILITY
Generally larger and slow-moving.

CLAWS
While the biggest herbivores had no claws to speak of, some smaller plant-eating dinosaurs are believed to have had sharp claws. These were most likely used for grasping, digging and piercing.

DIGESTIVE SYSTEM
Some herbivores would swallow stones to grind down the large quantity of plant matter in their big stomachs and intestines. Some of them may even have evolved fermentation chambers that helped them to digest their food.

MOVEMENT
Most herbivorous dinosaurs walked on all fours, but a few of the smaller ones – such as Hadrosaurus from the late Cretaceous Period – had bird-like hip bones that allowed them to stand up on their hind legs and run away from danger.

PROTECTIVE FEATURES
Because the herbivores could not outrun their powerful carnivorous cousins, they had to develop other ways of protecting themselves (bony spikes, armoured plates, clubbed tails and so on).

CARNIVORES

BRAIN
Generally larger relative to the size of their body, which may have been linked to their need to hunt prey at speed.

MOUTH
Long, sharp (often serrated) teeth designed for tearing easily through flesh, plus extremely powerful jaws that moved up and down rather than side to side. T-Rex, for example, had a bite that was three times as strong as a lion's!

NECK
In proportion with their bodies. A long neck would have made it much more difficult for them to hunt.

SIZE AND AGILITY
Generally smaller and fast-moving.

CLAWS
Sharp and pointy, to pierce and rip apart prey.

DIGESTIVE SYSTEM
Generally smaller than that of the herbivores, with lots of acidic digestive juices to aid the rapid breakdown of their meaty meal before it began to rot!

MOVEMENT
The predatory dinosaurs were generally bipedal. This means that they walked on two legs, which helped them to outrun their plant-eating prey.

PROTECTIVE FEATURES
As fearsome predators with sharp teeth and claws and an ultra-powerful bite, the carnivorous dinosaurs did not require too much additional protection.

FAMILY TIES

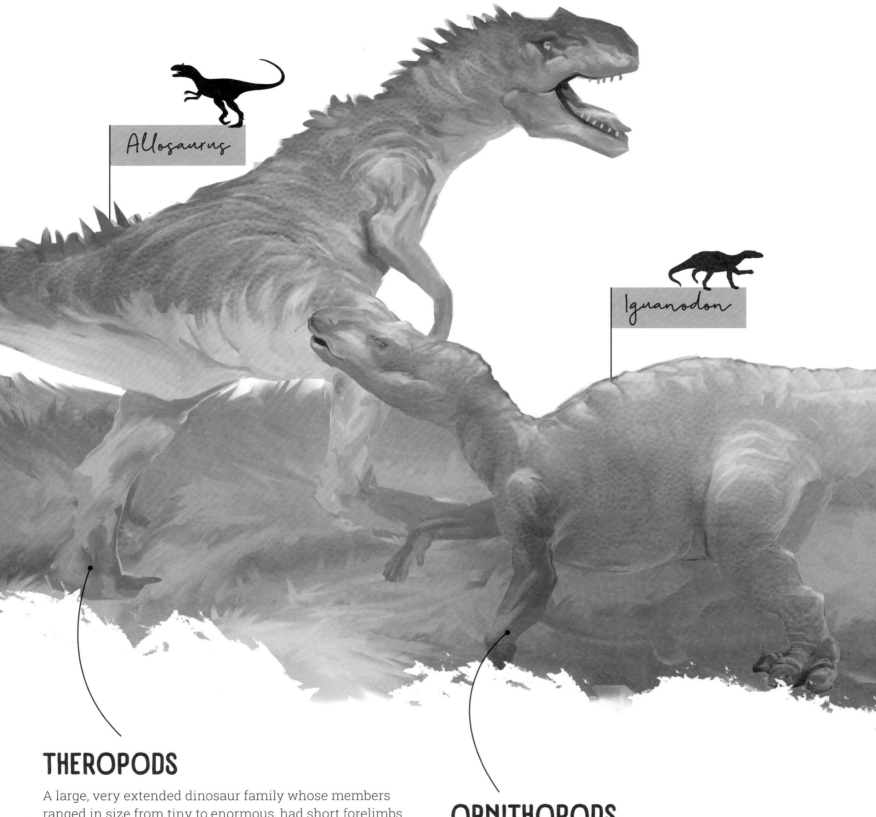

Allosaurus

Iguanodon

THEROPODS

A large, very extended dinosaur family whose members ranged in size from tiny to enormous, had short forelimbs and walked or ran upright on their strong hind limbs. The largest species were carnivorous, while some of the smaller ones ate plants.

Some family members
Late Triassic: Coelophysis
Early Jurassic: Dilophosaurus
Late Jurassic: Allosaurus, Archaeopteryx, Compsognathus
Early Cretaceous: Deinonychus, Giganotosaurus
Late Cretaceous: Gallimimus, Oviraptor, Tyrannosaurus

ORNITHOPODS

A family of peaceful, medium-sized herbivores that could walk on two legs, although probably grazed on all fours. The duck-billed dinosaurs belonged to this category.

Some family members
Early Jurassic: Heterodontosaurus
Late Jurassic: Agilisaurus
Early Cretaceous: Iguanodon
Late Cretaceous: Pachycephalosaurus, Parasaurolophus

SAUROPODS

A family of extremely large, long-necked, herbivorous dinosaurs that walked on four legs and flourished during the Jurassic and Cretaceous periods.

Some family members
Late Triassic: Melanorosaurus
Early Jurassic: Barapasaurus
Late Jurassic: Brachiosaurus, Diplodocus
Early Cretaceous: Austrosaurus
Late Cretaceous: Argentinosaurus

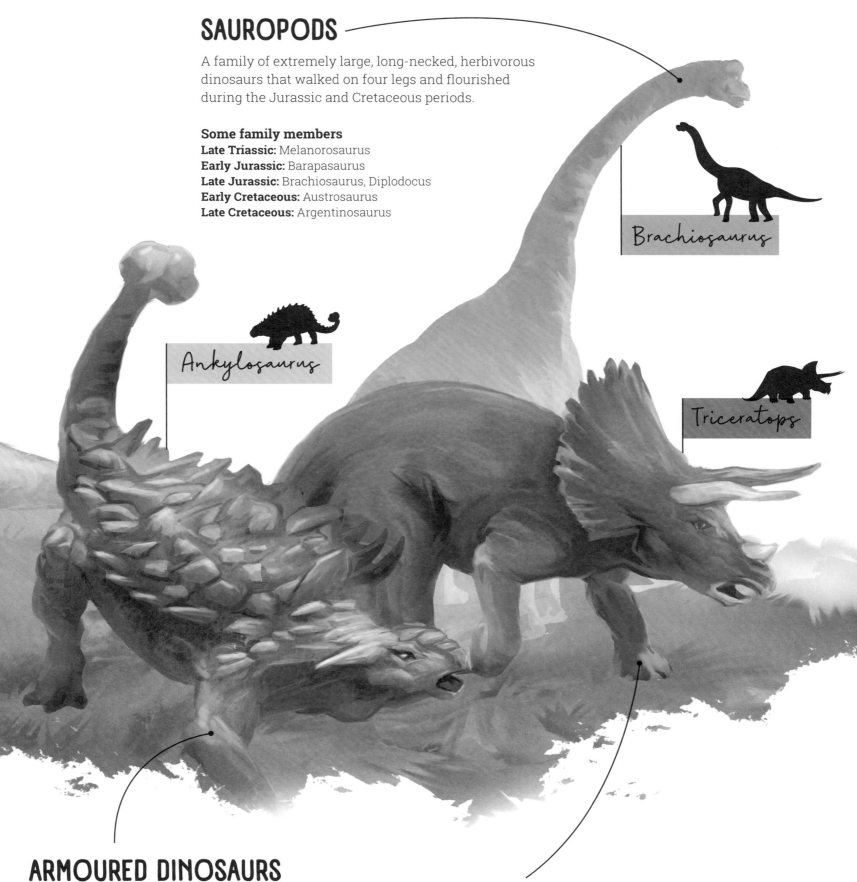

Brachiosaurus

Ankylosaurus

Triceratops

ARMOURED DINOSAURS

A class of medium-sized herbivores that walked on all fours and had some kind of body armour. Both the ankylosaurs and the stegosaurs belonged to this family.

Some family members
Early Jurassic: Scelidosaurus
Late Jurassic: Kentrosaurus, Stegosaurus
Early Cretaceous: Gastonia, Sauropelta
Late Cretaceous: Ankylosaurus

CERATOPSIANS

Four-legged, herbivorous dinosaurs with beaked mouths that lived during the Cretaceous Period. Many of them also sported elaborate neck frills and/or horns.

Some family members
Early Cretaceous: Archaeoceratops, Psittacosaurus
Late Cretaceous: Bagaceratops, Centrosaurus, Triceratops

DINO LIFE

Fossils – including fossilised tracks and footprints – give us strong clues about dinosaur lifestyles; not only what they ate, but how (and how much) they moved about and whether they lived alone or in groups.

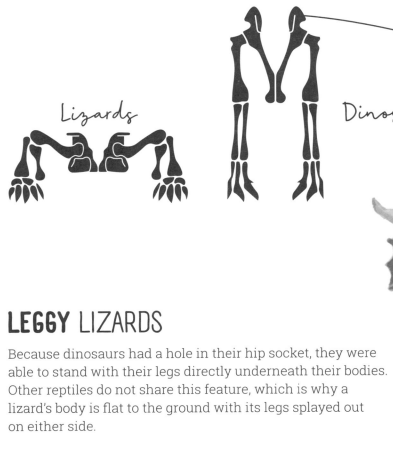

Lizards

Dinosaurs

LEGGY LIZARDS

Because dinosaurs had a hole in their hip socket, they were able to stand with their legs directly underneath their bodies. Other reptiles do not share this feature, which is why a lizard's body is flat to the ground with its legs splayed out on either side.

CUMBERSOME CREATURES?

For a long time, dinosaurs were seen as large, awkward creatures that found it difficult to move about. While it's true that many of the biggest plant-eaters walked around slowly on all fours, their predatory cousins could walk upright. In fact, we now know that many dinosaurs were very agile, able to run quickly on two legs.

HERD MENTALITY

Like many wild animals today, some dinosaurs were undoubtedly solitary. However, we now believe that certain species of horned dinosaurs, such as Triceratops, may have lived in large herds – possibly for protection; possibly to help raise their young. For a palaeontologist, nothing is more exciting than finding a big collection of dinosaur fossils together in the same place! Thanks to such discoveries, there is even some evidence that big carnivores such as Giganotosaurus may have lived in family groups.

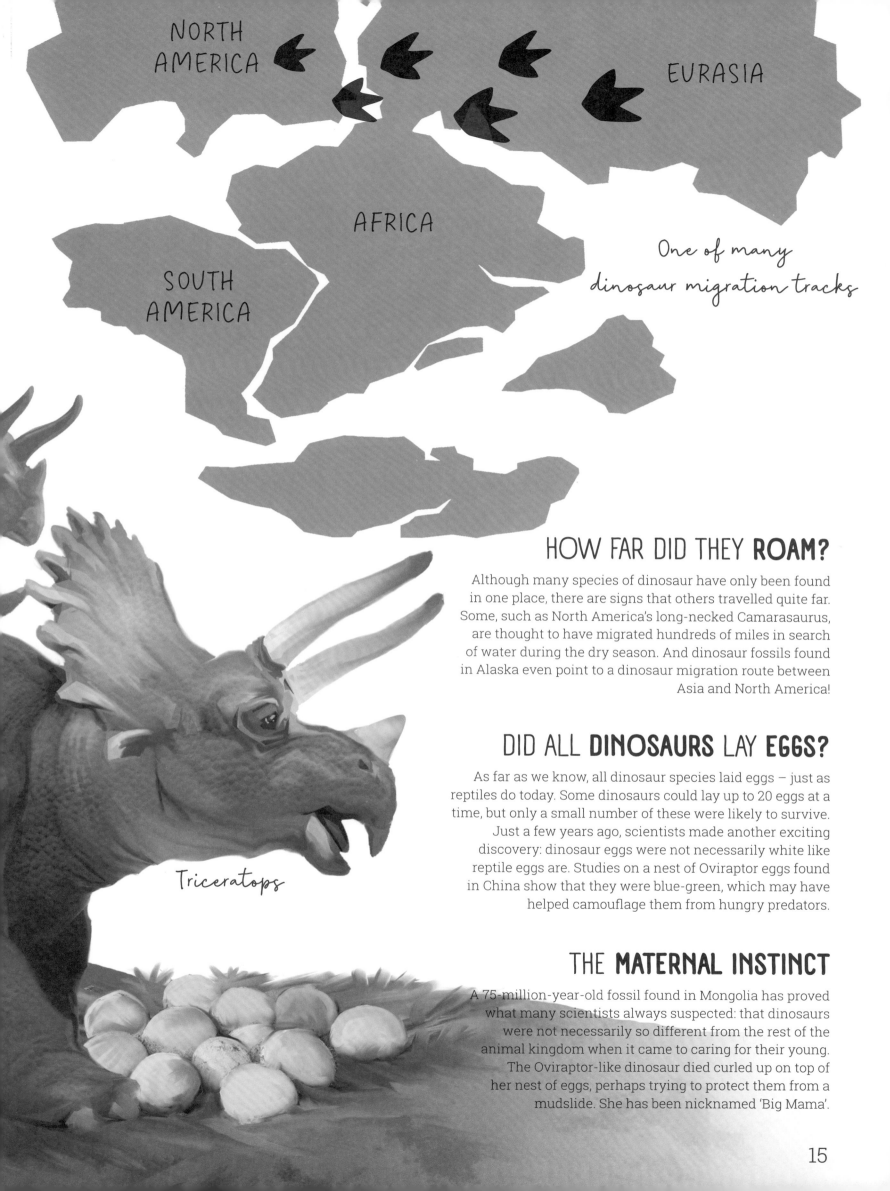

NORTH AMERICA

EURASIA

AFRICA

SOUTH AMERICA

One of many dinosaur migration tracks

Triceratops

HOW FAR DID THEY **ROAM?**

Although many species of dinosaur have only been found in one place, there are signs that others travelled quite far. Some, such as North America's long-necked Camarasaurus, are thought to have migrated hundreds of miles in search of water during the dry season. And dinosaur fossils found in Alaska even point to a dinosaur migration route between Asia and North America!

DID ALL **DINOSAURS** LAY **EGGS?**

As far as we know, all dinosaur species laid eggs – just as reptiles do today. Some dinosaurs could lay up to 20 eggs at a time, but only a small number of these were likely to survive. Just a few years ago, scientists made another exciting discovery: dinosaur eggs were not necessarily white like reptile eggs are. Studies on a nest of Oviraptor eggs found in China show that they were blue-green, which may have helped camouflage them from hungry predators.

THE **MATERNAL INSTINCT**

A 75-million-year-old fossil found in Mongolia has proved what many scientists always suspected: that dinosaurs were not necessarily so different from the rest of the animal kingdom when it came to caring for their young. The Oviraptor-like dinosaur died curled up on top of her nest of eggs, perhaps trying to protect them from a mudslide. She has been nicknamed 'Big Mama'.

DINOSAUR DEFENCES

If placid, plant-eating dinosaurs wanted to survive, they needed to come up with some good defence mechanisms to ward off those hungry carnivores! Dinosaurs that did not have any particularly noteworthy defence mechanisms probably found safety in numbers.

THERIZINOSAURUS

Not much is known about this dinosaur, which dates from the **late Cretaceous**, except that it had metre-long claws that may have been used for defence and grabbing vegetation.

ANKYLOSAURUS

This 4,000 kilogram herbivore from the **late Cretaceous** period was built like a tank, with tough body armour and an enormous tail club that could crush bones.

STEGOSAURUS

This **Jurassic** beast sported a set of massive, pointy spikes on its tail and a ridge of bony plates down its back. These plates may have looked dangerous, but they were probably too thin to defend it from attack. Its tail was its most powerful weapon.

BRACHIOSAURUS

The sheer size and strong tail of this **late Jurassic** dinosaur would have been enough to put off even the foolhardiest of predators.

DIPLODOCUS

At the end of the **Jurassic** period, this 'gentle giant' was able to use its unimaginably long tail like a whip if ever any carnivore made the ill-considered decision to attack.

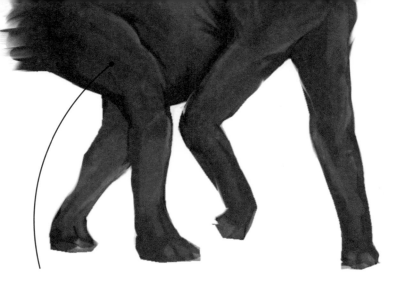

BRONTOMERUS

This recently discovered species dating from the **early Cretaceous** was named after its 'thunder thighs'. It was a big sauropod that could give quite a kick!

TRICERATOPS

Can you imagine a face-off between a Tyrannosaurus and a Triceratops in the **Cretaceous** period? That must have been one of the most awe-inspiring battles of all time! Triceratops would hold its own thanks to its enormous bulk, incredible strength and massive horned skull.

PACHYCEPHALOSAURUS

Some **70 million years ago**, this herbivorous dinosaur would use the 25 centimetre-thick dome on top of its skull as a battering ram – often in battles over a mate, but undoubtedly also to protect itself!

SAUROPELTA

This dinosaur dating from the **early Cretaceous** was well-protected in its bony, studded armour, which would have all but prevented a predator from getting its teeth in; it also had some alarmingly long shoulder spines!

HYPACROSAURUS

Another interesting defence mechanism was displayed by this duck-billed dinosaur from **70 million years ago**: Hypacrosaurus grew at lightning speed! It reached full size in just 10 to 12 years (about 3 times quicker than T-Rex).

SPEED

It is incredibly difficult to estimate a dinosaur's top speed when all we have to go on are a few fossils and some footprint tracks in mud – and nobody runs their fastest in mud! This said, it seems reasonable to suppose that a heavy species would have moved more slowly than a lighter one.

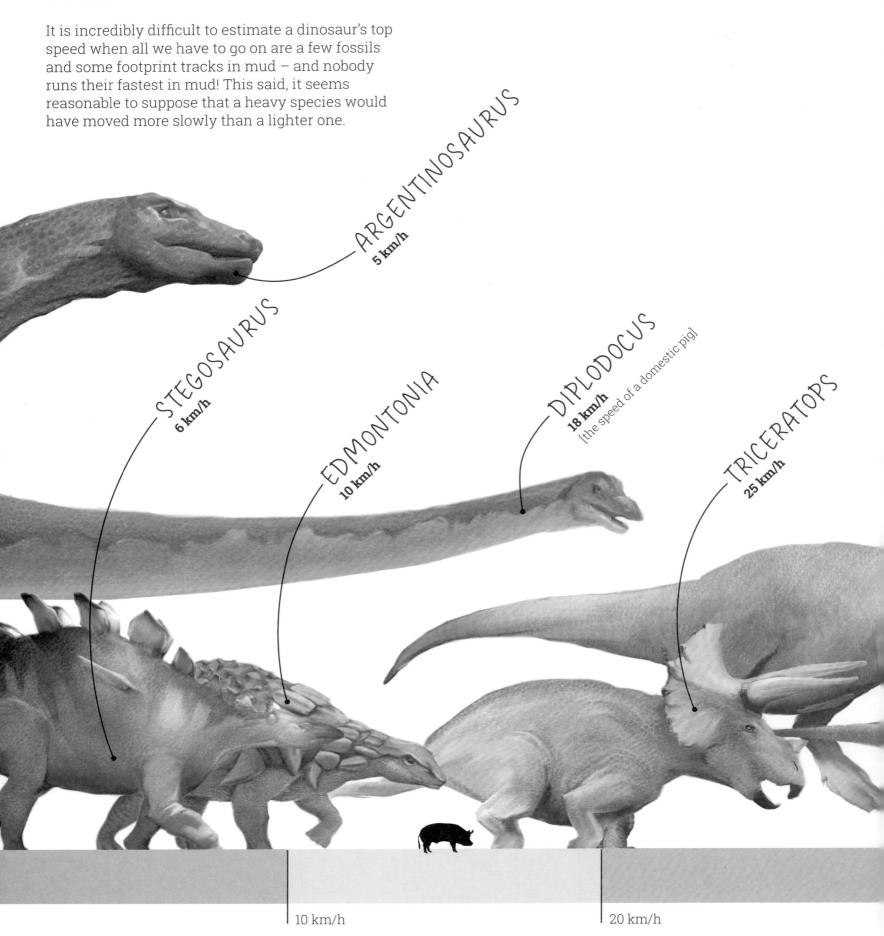

ARGENTINOSAURUS
5 km/h

STEGOSAURUS
6 km/h

EDMONTONIA
10 km/h

DIPLODOCUS
18 km/h
[the speed of a domestic pig]

TRICERATOPS
25 km/h

10 km/h

20 km/h

It is clear from the estimated top speeds below that
no dinosaur would have been able to outrun a car...
or a cheetah for that matter!
(A cheetah can reach a top speed of 112 km/h!)

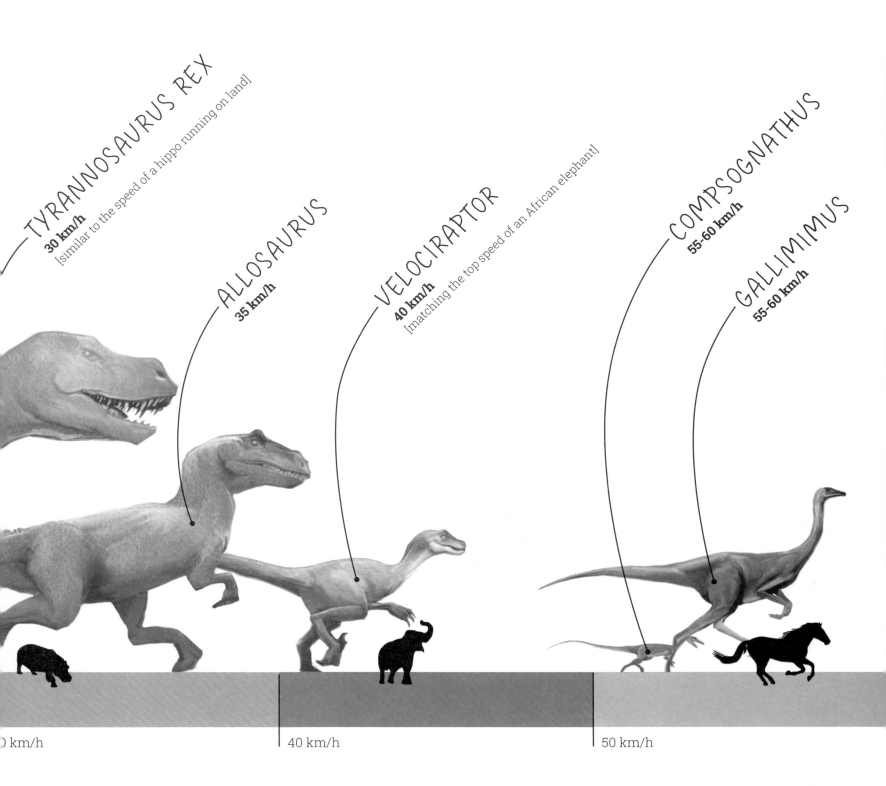

TYRANNOSAURUS REX
30 km/h
[similar to the speed of a hippo running on land]

ALLOSAURUS
35 km/h

VELOCIRAPTOR
40 km/h
[matching the top speed of an African elephant]

COMPSOGNATHUS
55-60 km/h

GALLIMIMUS
55-60 km/h

0 km/h

40 km/h

50 km/h

Tiny Compsognathus (3 kilograms) and giant ostrich-like Gallimimus
(200 kilograms), both theropods, are thought to be among the fastest dinosaurs
ever. They could both reach the speed of a tiger – or a galloping racehorse!

HEAD TO HEAD

STEGOSAURUS

A tiny, pointed head — which was extremely small in relation to its large body — carried close to the ground thanks to its short front legs.

TRICERATOPS

Unlike Stegosaurus, Triceratops' skull was large relative to its body. It also had a thick, bony frill at the back of its head. Despite the meaning of its name ('three-horned face'), Triceratops only had two real horns. The third, the small one at the end of its nose, was made from a similar material to our fingernails, so wouldn't have been much use in a fight!

STYRACOSAURUS

A relative of Triceratops, Styracosaurus had a long nose horn and an enormous frill crowned with formidable spikes.

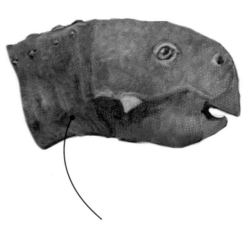

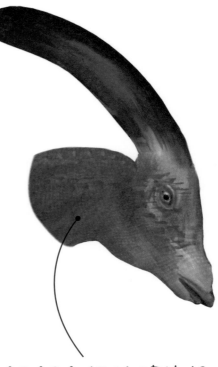

PSITTACOSAURUS

This plant-eater from the early Cretaceous Period had a tortoise-like head with a parrot-like beak and small horns on both cheeks.

HETERODONTOSAURUS

Unlike most reptiles, Heterodontosaurus had three different types of teeth... including a set of sharp canines. Could this plant-eater have actually been an omnivore?

PARASAUROLOPHUS

This duck-billed dinosaur had an elaborate head crest in the form of a long tube that projected out the back of its skull. The crest was hollow, with tubes running through it from the nostrils before returning into the skull. This crest may have improved the dinosaur's sense of smell, been used to produce sounds or helped in regulating body temperature. So many possibilities!

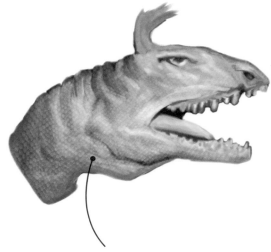

PACHYCEPHALOSAURUS
Known for its unusually thick skull, which may have been used for ramming other dinosaurs!

DILOPHOSAURUS
This North American predator sported a double head crest that may have helped the males to attract a mate.

CRYOLOPHOSAURUS
This 'frozen crested lizard', living in what is now Antarctica, had a small curved crest on its head, probably purely for display.

BARYONYX
This fish-eating dinosaur had the mouth of a crocodile, with nostrils set quite far back towards the eyes. This meant that it could dip its long snout into the water to catch fish.

FEATHERS VERSUS SCALES

What covered the surface of dinosaurs' skin has been debated ever since the first dinosaur fossil was discovered hundreds of years ago – and palaeontologists are still not sure today!

FEATHERED FRIENDS

We have known for a long time that some dinosaurs had feathers of one kind or another, such as the late Jurassic's pint-sized flying carnivore Archaeopteryx and the early Cretacean Psittacosaurus, which had porcupine-like bristles on its tail. However, over the last few decades, research has suggested that all dinosaurs may actually have had some kind of coat, whether it was soft or bristly.

COLD AND CLAMMY OR WARM AND DRY?

Since very few pieces of fossilised dino skin have been found, researchers have had to piece together other clues to work out what it might have looked like – such as fossils that formed where dinosaur skin had once pressed against mud, leaving an impression. Scientists believe that most dinosaurs were covered in small, non-overlapping scales that would have felt a bit bumpy and knobbly. And because there were no sweat glands in their skin, they would probably have been warm and dry to the touch.

EVEN THE **MIGHTY T-REX?**

Well, perhaps not. While earlier tyrannosaurs clearly had some kind of downy covering, it now seems unlikely that the King of the Carnivores had much more than a handful of feathers on its back. Tyrannosaurus may have shed the feathers sported by its earlier, smaller relatives as it was so big that it no longer needed them to keep warm. We also believe that T-Rex lived on the open plains instead of in shady forests – so it probably needed more help cooling down than it did warming up!

BODY ARMOUR

Some dinosaurs – the ankylosaurs – were covered in bony growths or plates called 'osteoderms' that grew from within the skin. Nobody is entirely sure what purpose these growths served. Certainly, they would have provided the dinosaur with a protective covering – a bit like a knight's armour – but they may also have helped it to regulate its body temperature or to attract a mate.

WHAT **COLOUR** WERE THE DINOSAURS?

The short answer is that we don't know. However, many modern-day reptiles and birds are brightly coloured, so there is no reason to believe that all the dinosaurs were brown or grey, as they are often depicted. They may even have been masters of camouflage!

23

BACK TO BACK

Size: 7 metres long, 1.8 metres tall, 5,000 kilograms
Period: late Cretaceous
(74 − 67 million years ago)
Found: Canada, USA

Ankylosaurus's flat body armour was covered in bony knobs down its back and spikes on its sides. It also wielded a heavy tail club.

STEGOSAURUS

Size: 9 metres long, 4 metres tall, 3,500 kilograms
Period: late Jurassic
(155 − 145 million years ago)
Found: USA

Stegosaurus is one of the best-known armoured dinosaurs. It had a double row of broad, upright plates all the way down its back as well as a spiked tail. Some scientists believe that its plates may have changed colour as a way of communicating with other members of the species.

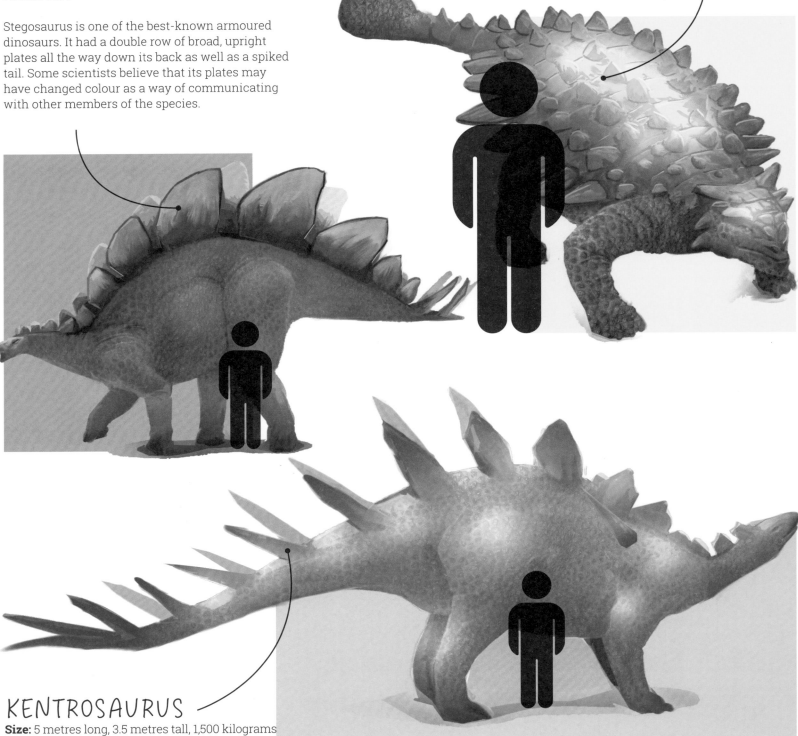

KENTROSAURUS

Size: 5 metres long, 3.5 metres tall, 1,500 kilograms
Period: late Jurassic
(155 − 150 million years ago)
Found: Tanzania

Another armoured dinosaur, Kentrosaurus also sported a series of double plates down its neck and back, but these became awe-inspiring spikes the further back they went. Its lengthy tail spikes were a powerful defensive weapon and it also had an intimidating spike on each shoulder.

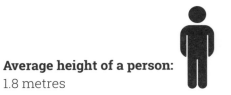

Average height of a person:
1.8 metres

24

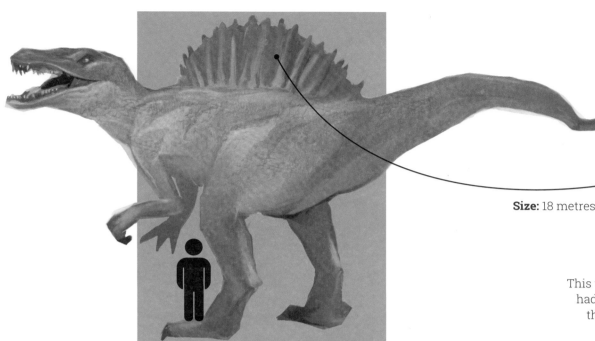

SPINOSAURUS

Size: 18 metres long, 7 metres tall, 7,000 kilograms
Period: late Cretaceous
(95 – 70 million years ago)
Found: Egypt, Morocco

This theropod, the tallest carnivore ever, had a two-metre-high 'sail' on its back, the purpose of which is still debated.

OURANOSAURUS

Size: 7 metres long, 3 metres tall, 3,000 kilograms
Period: early Cretaceous
(115 – 100 million years ago)
Found: Niger

Ouranosaurus was a herbivorous ornithopod with a hump-like spine down its back.

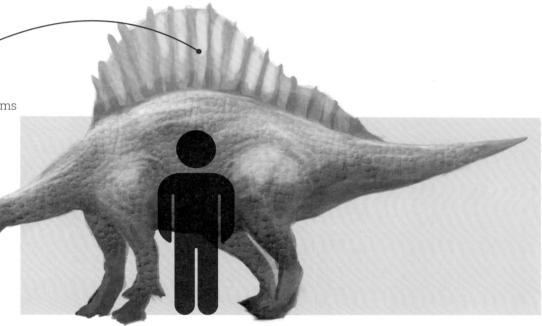

ACROCANTHOSAURUS

Size: 12 metres long, 4 metres tall, 6,000 kilograms
Period: early Cretaceous
(115 – 105 million years ago)
Found: Canada, USA

This theropod was given its name, meaning 'high-spined lizard', after the long spines that rose up along the entire length of its backbone. These spines are likely to have supported some kind of hump or short sail.

ALONGSIDE THE DINOSAURS

The dinosaurs may have ruled the prehistoric roost, but they were certainly not alone in it – they were accompanied by a whole host of impressive creatures that roamed the skies above and the waters below.

PTEROSAURS

The pterosaurs were flying reptiles that evolved on a separate branch of the family tree to the dinosaurs. They were the first animals, apart from insects, to evolve the ability to fly (not simply glide). They ranged in size from the Dimorphodon (which lived in the late Triassic Period and was about the size of a large crow) to the late Cretacean Pteranodon (with its whopping 6-metre wingspan).

Pteranodon

Plesiosaurus

PLESIOSAURS

This group of long-necked marine reptiles (or 'sea monsters'!) co-existed with the dinosaurs from the late Triassic until the late Cretaceous Period. One of the earliest plesiosaurs was Plesiosaurus, which was around 4.5 metres long with a long neck and a short tail. While some plesiosaurs had extremely long necks and small heads, others had huge, elongated heads but shorter necks. Plesiosaurs were able to use their long necks to sneak up on their fishy prey. They also gave birth to live young, unlike most reptiles.

INSECTS

Giant dragonflies, millipedes and cockroaches inhabited the planet once upon a time – but not during the Mesozoic Era. They were all wiped out either before or during the mass extinction that brought in the Mesozoic Era. Fossil evidence suggests that the insects that co-existed with the dinosaurs were not, in fact, very different from the insects we know today – perhaps a little larger, but not enormous. They included ancient butterflies (lacewings), stick insects and scarab beetles that fed on dinosaur dung!

Dicynodont

Juramaia

Triassic Period	**Jurassic** Period	**Cretaceous** Period	
252 mya	201 mya	145 mya	66 mya

EARLY MAMMALS

For a long time, scientists believed that the only mammals to survive the mass extinction that marked the start of the Mesozoic Era were tiny creatures that lived on insects and kept under cover! Yet the recent discovery of an elephant-sized fossil in Poland has cast doubt on this theory. The creature is a giant herbivorous dicynodont, a distant relative of today's mammals. It dates from the early Triassic Period, so would have co-existed with some of the earliest dinosaurs. A tiny shrew-like creature called Juramaia, which dates to 160 million years ago, is the earliest-known direct ancestor of 'placental mammals'.

ORIGIN OF BIRDS

Perhaps surprisingly, the magpie in your garden did not evolve from the pterosaurs, but actually from the 'theropods' – the family of dinosaurs to which T-Rex belonged!

BIPEDAL LOCOMOTION

It is now clear that some of the oldest dinosaurs shared many features in common with modern birds – features such as the ability to walk on two legs.

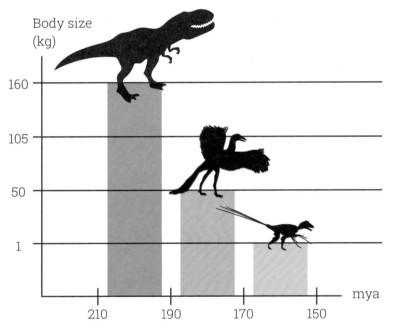

EVER-DECREASING SIZE

Sometime during the Jurassic, a branch of carnivorous theropods began to shrink. This evolutionary process gave rise to Archaeopteryx (one of the first theropods to take to the skies), Deinonychus and Velociraptor, among others. Getting smaller had a real evolutionary advantage: smaller carnivores could climb trees and even glide. They also required less food and could find shelter more easily, hence they managed to survive the mass extinction that wiped out most of the dinosaurs!

FEATHERS

Studies suggest that many dinosaurs had some kind of insulating layer of feathers or bristles. Over time, however, theropods such as Oviraptor evolved longer feathers on their short arms. With arms this short, they would never have been able to fly, so scientists believe they used the feathers to shield the eggs in their nests. Eventually these feathers began to resemble those of today's birds, which are perfectly adapted to flight.

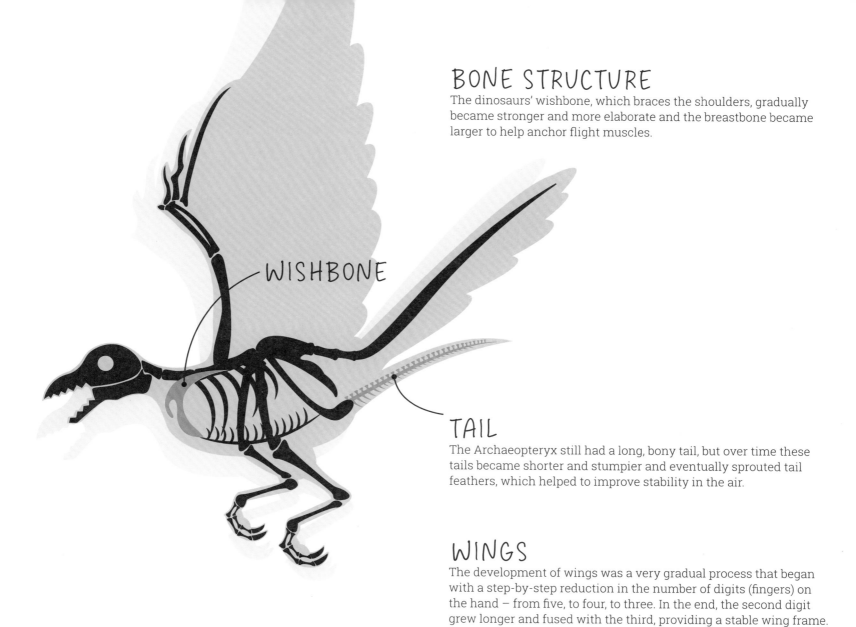

BONE STRUCTURE

The dinosaurs' wishbone, which braces the shoulders, gradually became stronger and more elaborate and the breastbone became larger to help anchor flight muscles.

WISHBONE

TAIL

The Archaeopteryx still had a long, bony tail, but over time these tails became shorter and stumpier and eventually sprouted tail feathers, which helped to improve stability in the air.

WINGS

The development of wings was a very gradual process that began with a step-by-step reduction in the number of digits (fingers) on the hand – from five, to four, to three. In the end, the second digit grew longer and fused with the third, providing a stable wing frame.

From digits to wings

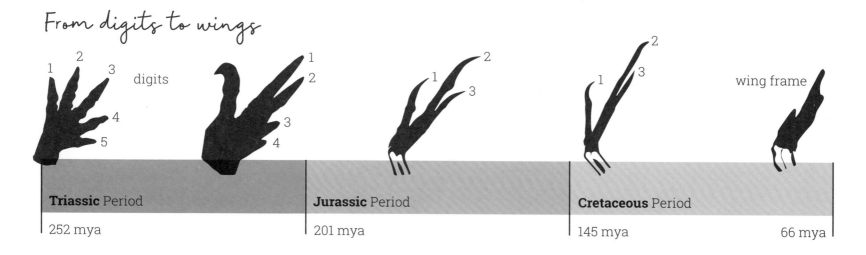

digits

1
2
3
4
5

1
2
3
4

1
2
3

1
3
2

wing frame

Triassic Period	**Jurassic** Period	**Cretaceous** Period
252 mya	201 mya	145 mya 66 mya

BEAK

150 million years ago, Archaeopteryx still had a snout filled with reptilian teeth. A number of the smaller theropods then went through a series of evolutionary steps that led to the loss of teeth and the development of a keratin beak.

OCEANS DEEP

ICHTHYOSAURS
Dolphin-like marine reptiles that multiplied rapidly during the Triassic Period and died out before the dinosaurs did (around 90 million years ago).

Shonisaurus
Period: late Triassic – **Length**: 15 metres
Interestingly, an adult Shonisaurus had no teeth.

Shastasaurus
Period: late Triassic – **Length**: 21 metres
It was the largest-ever marine reptile.

Eurhinosaurus
Period: early Jurassic – **Length**: 6 metres
Its upper jaw protruded, making it look a lot like a giant swordfish.

PLESIOSAURS
Marine reptiles that evolved during the Triassic Period and met their downfall 66 million years ago, along with the dinosaurs.

Plesiosaurus
Period: early Jurassic – **Length**: 4.5 metres
Surprisingly, Plesiosaurus may have come ashore to lay its eggs, like today's sea turtle.

Pliosaurus
Period: late Jurassic – **Length**: 15 metres
It had the strongest bite of any known animal – many times stronger than that of T-Rex, which it could have gobbled up in one go… if they had been alive at the same time.

Kronosaurus
Period: early Cretaceous – **Length**: 12 metres
It had a huge, elongated head (accounting for almost a third of its length!), but a relatively short neck.

Elasmosaurus
Period: late Cretaceous – **Length**: 13 metres
It had an exceptionally long neck (accounting for half of its body length!), but only a small head.

Leptostyrax
Period: early Cretaceous – **Length**: 10 metres
This long shark was a cousin of today's great white.

Sarcosuchus
Period: early Cretaceous – **Length**: 9 metres
This sea crocodile was the largest crocodile to ever live – and it never stopped growing!

Mosasaurus
Period: late Cretaceous – **Length**: 17 metres
This predatory lizard's streamlined body and flippers enabled it to cut through the water at great speed.

SMALLER SEA LIFE
The Jurassic and Cretaceous periods were home to ammonites (extinct shelled relatives of today's squid), starfish, sponges and sea urchins, among other smaller sea creatures.

FOSSIL FAQ

WHAT IS **PALAEONTOLOGY**?

A very difficult word to spell! Palaeontology is the study of fossils – the remains or traces of creatures that lived in a previous age – in order to better understand the history of life on Earth.

HOW DO **FOSSILS FORM**?

Most of our fossils are stone relics of plants and animals that were completely buried in sand, mud or volcanic ash very soon after they died. This is why almost all of them are found at the bottom of the sea or very near a lake or river that once flooded: they sank into the sand or mud, which not only put them under immense pressure but also blocked out the air, helping to slow down the rate of decomposition. Another type of fossil forms when small insects or plants get trapped in sticky tree resin, which then hardens.

DOES **EVERYTHING** EVENTUALLY **FOSSILISE**?

No. In fact, very few things do as it is rare for all the right conditions to be in place to allow this to happen. Most things that die simply rot away, leaving no trace – and therefore no clues for future generations to find.

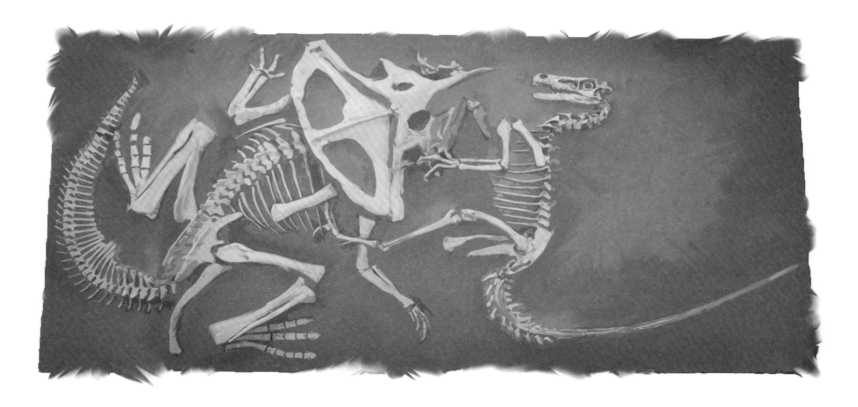

WHAT ARE SOME OF THE **MOST INTERESTING FOSSILS** EVER FOUND?

While most fossils are tiny, individual fragments of bone or small shellfish, palaeontologists have made some mind-blowing discoveries too: two dinosaurs literally mid-battle, a mother dinosaur sitting on a nest full of eggs and a snake on the verge of swallowing a baby dinosaur!

WHAT CAN WE **LEARN** FROM **FOSSILS**?

Even the smallest of fossils can give us big clues about life in prehistoric times. They give us a sense of what extinct creatures might have looked like, where they lived, how far they travelled, what they ate, how many babies they had, whether they lived in groups, and so on... Just imagine – if it weren't for fossils, we would have had no idea dinosaurs ever existed!

FOSSIL FORMS

BODY FOSSILS

Fossilised bones, teeth, claws, shells of sea creatures, unhatched eggs and so on all belong to the category of 'body fossils' – in other words, they are actual fossilised remains.

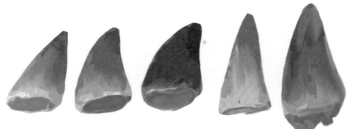

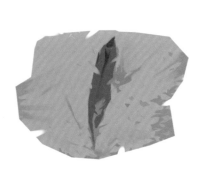

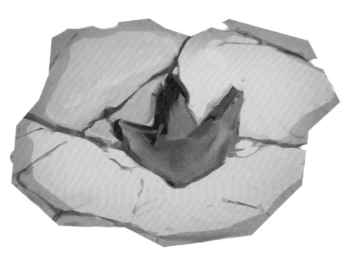

TRACE FOSSILS

Trace fossils are fossils that tell us more about what a creature was like without actually being the creature in question. For example, mud imprints of feathers, skin or footprints and even fossilised burrows or nests.

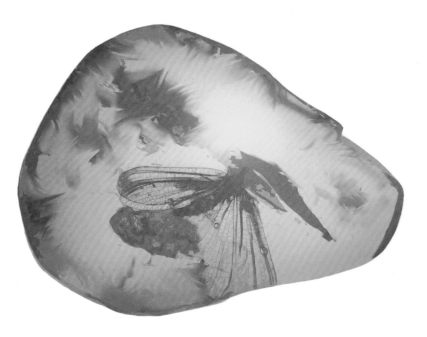

RESIN FOSSILS

These form when a plant, insect or other organism becomes trapped in sticky tree resin, which then hardens to form amber. The really exciting thing about these fossils is that they are completely intact specimens, including soft tissue, which have not turned to stone!

COPROLITES

Coprolites are fossilised poo! These fossils are very rare as dung generally decomposes very rapidly. However, the samples that have been found are really valuable to researchers as they tell us which animals lived where and what they ate. One particularly exciting specimen of Tyrannosaurus poo found in Canada, for example, contains the ground-up bones of a young dinosaur!

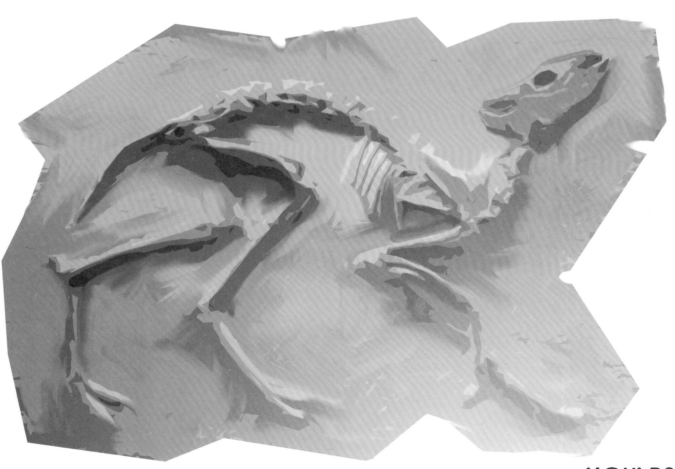

MOULDS AND CASTS

Some fossils look just like the bone (or shell or other object) they represent, but they are actually an ancient model of it instead. This happens when the bone has dissolved, leaving a bone-shaped hole in the layer of sediment it was buried in. This kind of natural 'mould' is still considered a fossil. And if this hole fills with a mineral-rich liquid, the minerals may crystallise and fill the void, creating a mineral fossil – known as a 'cast fossil' – in the shape of the original bone.

STANDARD **FOSSIL FORMATION**

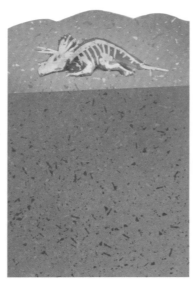

1. An animal dies.

2. The remains (mainly bones and teeth) are quickly buried in mud or sand.

3. Water seeps into any cavities, filling them with minerals that will turn to stone over time.

4. Many more layers of sediment build up on top, creating a lot of pressure and turning the lower layers to rock.

5. Thousands, if not millions, of years go by.

6. As the plates in the planet's crust gradually shift, lower layers of sedimentary rock are occasionally forced to the surface, bringing with them a wealth of history.

7. Elsewhere, weathering and erosion wear away at the surface layers of sedimentary rock, exposing the hidden treasure beneath.

8. The fossil is dug up – carefully! – and sent to the experts for analysis.

THE MESOZOIC
TIMELINE

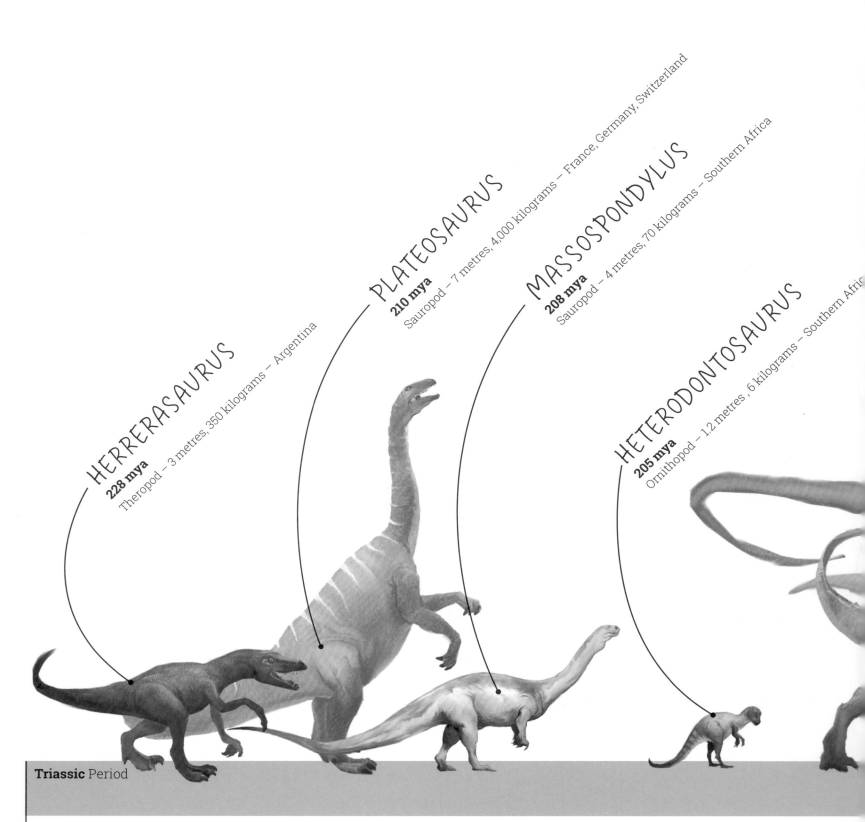

HERRERASAURUS
228 mya
Theropod – 3 metres, 350 kilograms – Argentina

PLATEOSAURUS
210 mya
Sauropod – 7 metres, 4,000 kilograms – France, Germany, Switzerland

MASSOSPONDYLUS
208 mya
Sauropod – 4 metres, 70 kilograms – Southern Africa

HETERODONTOSAURUS
205 mya
Ornithopod – 1.2 metres, 6 kilograms – Southern Afric

Triassic Period

252 mya

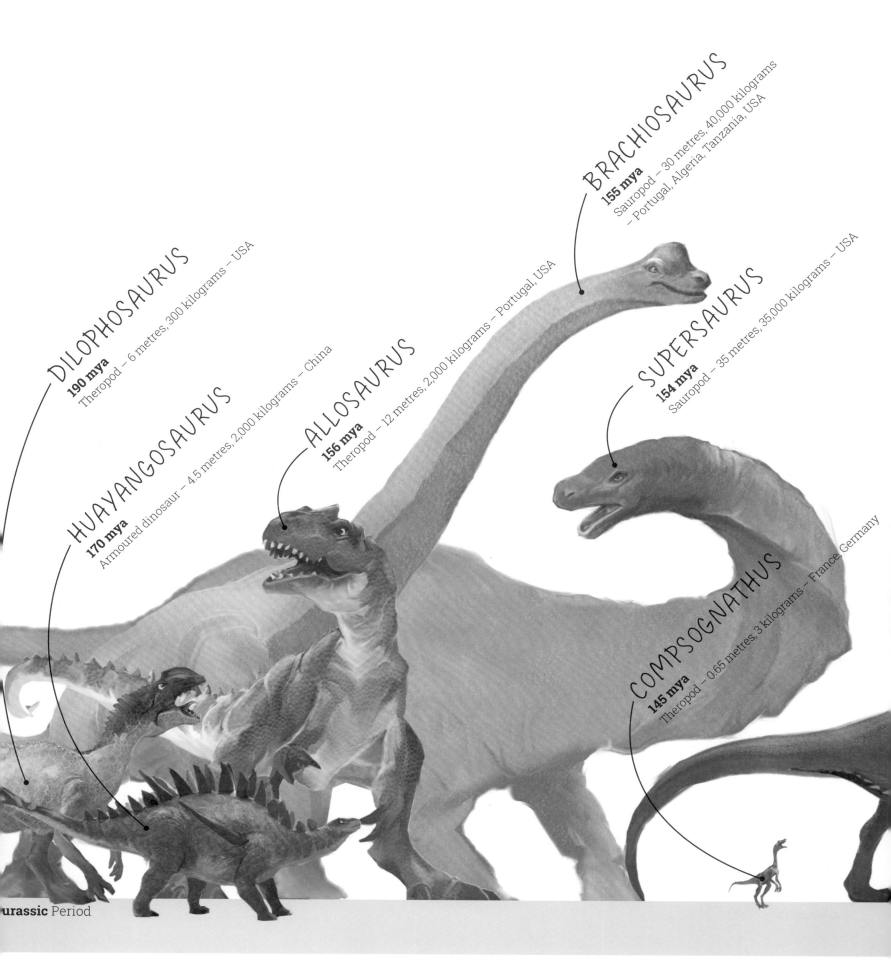

DILOPHOSAURUS
190 mya
Theropod – 6 metres, 300 kilograms – USA

HUAYANGOSAURUS
170 mya
Armoured dinosaur – 4.5 metres, 2,000 kilograms – China

ALLOSAURUS
156 mya
Theropod – 12 metres, 2,000 kilograms – Portugal, USA

BRACHIOSAURUS
155 mya
Sauropod – 30 metres, 40,000 kilograms
– Portugal, Algeria, Tanzania, USA

SUPERSAURUS
154 mya
Sauropod – 35 metres, 35,000 kilograms – USA

COMPSOGNATHUS
145 mya
Theropod – 0.65 metres, 3 kilograms – France Germany

urassic Period

01 mya

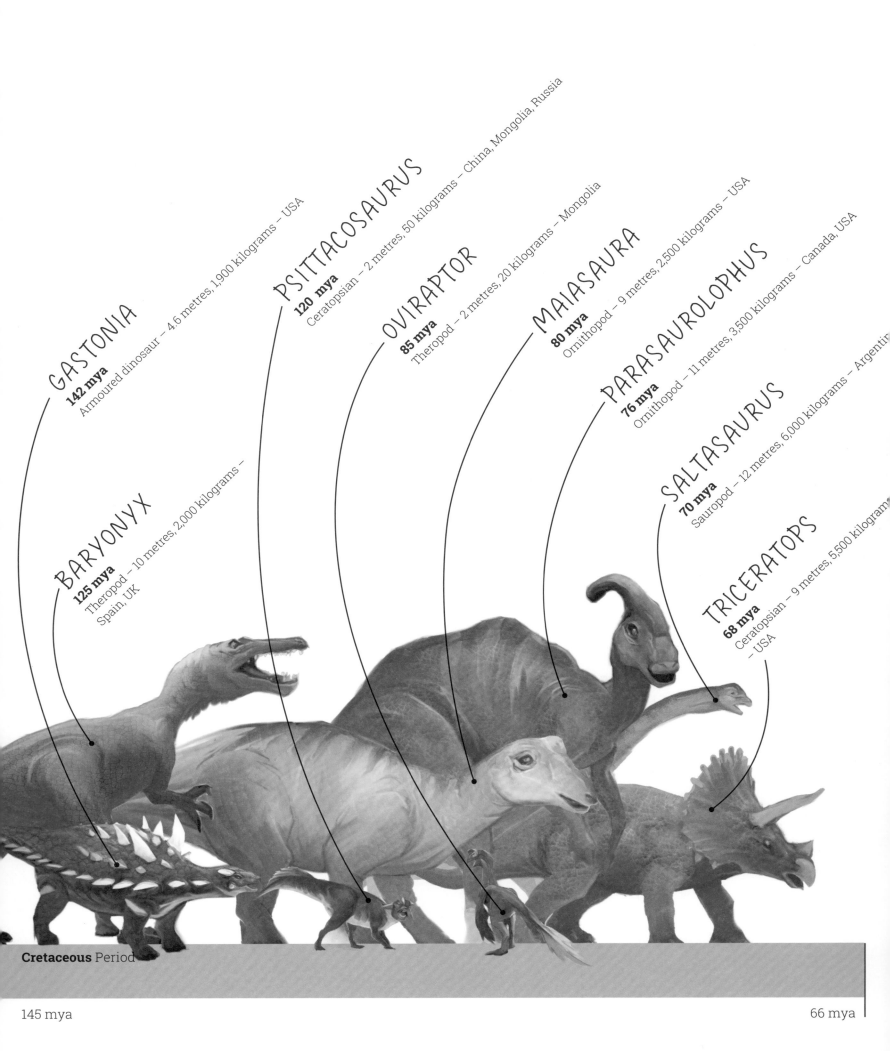

GASTONIA
142 mya
Armoured dinosaur – 4.6 metres, 1,900 kilograms – USA

BARYONYX
125 mya
Theropod – 10 metres, 2,000 kilograms –
Spain, UK

PSITTACOSAURUS
120 mya
Ceratopsian – 2 metres, 50 kilograms – China, Mongolia, Russia

OVIRAPTOR
85 mya
Theropod – 2 metres, 20 kilograms – Mongolia

MAIASAURA
80 mya
Ornithopod – 9 metres, 2,500 kilograms – USA

PARASAUROLOPHUS
76 mya
Ornithopod – 11 metres, 3,500 kilograms – Canada, USA

SALTASAURUS
70 mya
Sauropod – 12 metres, 6,000 kilograms – Argentin

TRICERATOPS
68 mya
Ceratopsian – 9 metres, 5,500 kilogram
– USA

Cretaceous Period

145 mya

66 mya

DIPLODOCUS

Size: 26 metres long, 20,000 kilograms
Diet: herbivore
Type: sauropod
Period: late Jurassic
(155 – 145 million years ago)
Found: USA

Among the longest dinosaurs, Diplodocus held its long tail and
neck horizontally, making it only slightly taller than a giraffe.

ARGENTINOSAURUS

Size: 35 metres long, 70,000 kilograms
Diet: herbivore
Type: sauropod
Period: late Cretaceous
(90 million years ago)
Found: Argentina

While this is slightly longer than the biggest blue whale (30 metres),
the blue whale comes in at more than double this weight!

IGUANODON

Size: 10 metres long, 4,000 kilograms
Diet: herbivore
Type: ornithopod
Period: early Cretaceous
       (140 – 110 million years ago)
Found: Belgium, UK, USA

Iguanodon could probably walk either on all fours or on two legs, standing no taller than an African elephant.

TYRANNOSAURUS REX

Size: 12 metres long, 7,000 kilograms
Diet: carnivore
Type: theropod
Period: late Cretaceous
       (68 – 66 million years ago)
Found: Canada, USA

T-Rex was the height of a giraffe, but far longer – and weighed as much as a large African elephant.

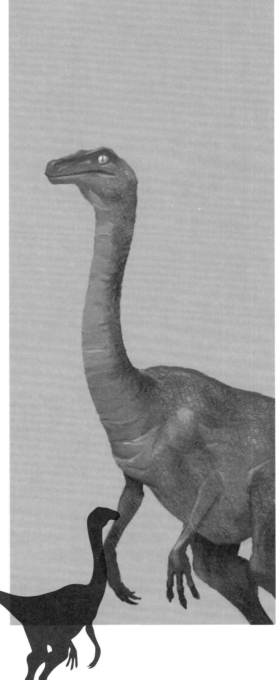

KENTROSAURUS

Size: 5 metres long, 1,500 kilograms
Diet: herbivore
Type: armoured dinosaur
Period: late Jurassic
      (155 – 150 million years ago)
Found: Tanzania

Kentrosaurus was a similar length to our white rhino, but a male white rhino is heavier.

GALLIMIMUS

Size: 6 metres long, 200 kilograms
Diet: omnivore
Type: theropod
Period: late Cretaceous
      (74 – 70 million years ago)
Found: Mongolia

Gallimimus looked a lot like an ostrich, but was at least twice the size.

STEGOSAURUS

Size: 9 metres long, 3,500 kilograms
Diet: herbivore
Type: armoured dinosaur
Period: late Jurassic
      (155 – 145 million years ago)
Found: USA

Stegosaurus was heavily built with a round back and its tail was held high in the air.

SIZING UP
DINOSAURS

ARCHAEOPTERYX

Size: 0.5 metres long, 1 kilogram
Diet: carnivore
Type: theropod
Period: late Jurassic
      (147 million years ago)
Found: Germany

Half reptile, half bird, Archaeopteryx
was the size of a modern chicken.

VELOCIRAPTOR

Size: 1.8 metres long, 15 kilograms
Diet: carnivore
Type: theropod
Period: late Cretaceous
      (74 – 70 million years ago)
Found: Mongolia

Though almost 2 metres long, in height the
Velociraptor was no taller than a turkey.

COELOPHYSIS

Size: 2 metres long, 25 kilograms
Diet: carnivore
Type: theropod
Period: late Triassic
      (225 – 190 million years ago)
Found: South Africa, USA, Zimbabwe

Coelophysis weighed about the same as
a dalmatian, but was about twice as long.